Poems Written and Collected by Arthur M. Pattison

and dedicated to my wonderful wife, Freda

WARNING:
If you decide to read ALOUD
These poems to a crowd,
Be sure to have a tissue near
To catch a falling tear.

Library of Congress Control Number: 2010907827
ISBN: Softcover 978-1-4535-1202-9
Hardcover 978-1-4535-1203-6

This book was printed in the United States of America.

To order additional copies of this book, contact:
Xlibris Corporation
1-888-795-4274
www.Xlibris.com
Orders@Xlibris.com

Seek the Lord
and His Strength;
Seek His Face Continually. Psalm 105:4

Here was a young man . . .

(One Solitary Life)

Born in an obscure village, the child of a peasant woman,
He worked in a carpenter shop, until he was thirty.
Then for three years he was an itinerant preacher.
He never married, he never raised a family,
He never owned a home, he never went to college,
He never wrote a book, he never held an office,
He never travelled more than 200 miles from his home.
He never did anything usually associated with greatness.
He had no credentials . . .

. . . but Himself.

While still a young man, public opinion turned against him;
When betrayed by a follower, his friends deserted him.
He was given a mockery of a trial, and nailed to a cross.
While dying, his executioners gambled for his clothes,
And after he died, he was laid in a borrowed grave.

****

Over nineteen centuries have come and gone,
Yet he remains the central figure of the human race,
And the leader in the column of progress; for
All the armies that have ever marched,
All the navies that have ever sailed,
All the parliaments that have ever sat,
All the kings that have ever reigned,
All put together, have not affected the life of man on earth
As has that . . .

. . . One Solitary Life.

Adapted by A. M. Pattison

This Is My Body . . .*

A Woman's Lament

(grieving the ban by many churches who do not ordain women
in spite of their service, many contributions and spiritual gifts)

After the labour ordained in the curse,
She'd rest by the manger and let her son nurse;
To shepherds and wise men who knelt in the mud,
She said, "This is my body, and this is my blood."

After she raised Him and taught all she could,
She wept from afar when He left home for good,
Then said, when she saw Him heal blind men with mud,
"Can He be my body, can He be my blood?"

After they whipped Him and hung Him on high,
She stayed by His side 'til He bid her goodbye,
And with eyes full of tears pouring out in a flood,
Cried, "This is my body, and this is my blood!"

After she washed Him and wrapped Him in myrrh,
She laid Him to rest in that cold sepulcher;
But when He arose she at last understood,
That "He was her body, and He was her blood!"

After she rises from each sacred meal,
She remembers how lonely and lost people feel;
But some STILL deny her a way to serve God,
To say, "THIS IS MY BODY, AND THIS IS MY BLOOD."

By Arthur M. Pattison

*The author has set this poem to music, and is happy to share
it with anyone who writes to him at Frameables@hotmail.com.

The Cross In My Pocket

I carry a cross in my pocket,
A simple reminder to me
Of the fact that I am a Christian
No matter where I may be.

This little cross is not magic,
Nor is it a good luck charm;
It isn't meant to protect me
From every physical harm.

It's not for identification,
For all the world to see;
It's simply an understanding
Between my Saviour and me.

When I put my hand in my pocket
To bring out a coin or key,
The cross is there to remind me
Of the price He paid for me.

It reminds me too, to be thankful
For my blessings day by day,
And to strive to serve Him better
In all that I do and say.

It's also a daily reminder
Of the peace and comfort I share
With all who acknowledge my Master
And give themselves to His care.

So, I carry a cross in my pocket
Reminding no one but me,
That Jesus Christ is Lord of my life
Because He has set me free!

Adapted by A. M. Pattison

My Dearest Wife

I go to work and pay the bills,
And mow the grass and such,
But when it comes to being on time.
I know that I'm not much.

I usually bought you flowers
On every special day.
And hoped that they would make-up
For words I could not say.

I told you once I'd love you
Until the end of time,
And would always let you know
If I ever changed my mind.

Life goes on, the days go by,
The months turn into years;
Some are filled with laughter,
Some are filled with tears.

But there's one thing that's never changed
And that's my love for you.
Although I don't express it well,
It's honest and it's true !

And now I list, with pen in hand,
My blessings, big and small,
And realize that knowing you
Is the greatest prize of all !

Adapted by A. M. Pattison
after a poem by Roy Harris

Parents: The First Bible Children Read

by Arthur M. Pattison

Parents are the first fragrance of God children breathe,
The first touch of God they feel,
The first voice of God they hear,
The first face of God they see,
The first fruits of God they taste, and
The first image of God they follow.

For, if children live with ridicule they learn to criticize,
With criticism comes condemnation,
With condemnation comes guilt,
With guilt comes anger,
With anger comes fighting,
With fighting comes violence, and
With violence comes DEATH; but . . .

If children live with encouragement they learn confidence,
With confidence comes respect for others,
With respect for others comes fairness,
With fairness comes justice,
With justice comes security,
With security comes love, and
With love comes LIFE.

God's "Special Child"

(for 'Special Parents')

A plea went out through heaven and earth,
"It's time again for a special birth,
For a special child who' ll need much love,"
Said angels to the Lord above.

"His progress may seem very slow,
Accomplishments he may not show;
And he will need some extra care
From all the folks he meets down there."

"He may not run or laugh or play,
His thoughts might seem to drift away.
In many ways he won't adapt,
And some will call him 'handicapped'."

"But You make babies, - not mistakes,
In the image of God each soul awakes;
And though he' ll need some special care,
He' ll be their 'Angel Unaware'."

"So let's be careful where he's sent,
We want his life to be content.
Please Lord, help find the parents who
Will do this sacred job for you."

"They may not know it right away, -
The leading role they're asked to play;
But give them all the Love it takes, -
Assure them you don't make mistakes!"

"And soon they'll know the privilege given,
In caring for their gift from Heaven;
This precious charge, so meek and mild,
Is Heaven's very 'Special Child'."

Adapted by A. M. Pattison

The "Chosen" Child

Once there were two women
Who longed for you to come;
One you don't remember
And one you call your Mom.

One mother had to give you up,
T'was all that she could do;
The other prayed for a child in need, -
God led her straight to you.

The first one gave you Life itself,
With a set of lungs so strong;
The second taught you how to live,
And know what's right from wrong.

Two women with two different lives,
Each helped you as you grew;
Each one became your greatest fan
And craved the best for you.

Your father gave you something grand, -
Your nationality,
And a culture that would help you form
Your personality.

You second dad gave you a name
And helped you to mature,
By giving you the discipline
To build your character.

Most parents who desire a child
Get one they can't refuse;
But some are lucky for they get
To raise a child they choose !

"Grew I from genes or environment ?"
You ask the Lord above;
"You're the best of both my child, -
Just different kinds of Love."

Adapted by A. M. Pattison

Acceptance

"I have two A's," the young boy said,
His voice was filled with glee;
His father answered with a scowl,
"How come you don't have three?"

"I've washed and dried the dishes, Mom !"
The girl called from the door;
Her mother sighed and quickly said,
"And did you sweep the floor ? "

****

But now the Lord has changed our lives,
And called us from above;
We thank him for accepting us
And showing us his love.

We're learning to forgive ourselves
And not to work so hard
At trying to be perfect with
'No flies in our backyard.'

For if the Lord's accepted us
With all our lives a - clutter
The very least that we can do
Is try to love each other.

****

"I have two A's," the young boy said,
His voice was filled with glee;
His father smiled and said, "That's great,
I'm proud as proud can be ! "

"I've washed and dried the dishes, Mom !"
The girl called from the door;
Her mother held her close and said,
"Each day I love you more !"

Adapted by A. M. Pattison

When You Thought I Wasn't Looking

When I came home from Nursery school, as proud as I could be.
I handed you my painting to, see what you'd think of me;
I saw you take my painting to the 'frigerator door
And when I saw you tape it there, it made me paint some more.

When we went for a walk one day along some crowded streets,
We came across an alley cat, who'd not been fed for weeks;
And when I saw you nurture her, with all your loving care,
I felt how good it was to help, whenever I could share.

I always went to church with you, and to my Sunday school,
And that is where I learned about, the Bible's Golden Rule.
One day you lost your temper, - then admitted you were flawed,
And when I saw you kneel and pray, I knew there was a God.

One day I saw your face get red, and tears fell from you eyes.
And then I knew that when I'm sad, I need not hide my cries.
Because you helped me to be strong, and always cared for me,
I always tried to make you proud, and be all that I could be.

And now that you are old and gray, your body tired from working,
I thank you for the things I saw, when you thought I wasn't looking.

Adapted by A. M. Pattison
from a poem by Mary Rita Schilke Korzan

Dearest Mother

by Arthur M. Pattison

You brought me up so lovingly
With so much thought and care;
You set a fine example
To follow everywhere.

You did the things that counted,
The things I'm thankful for;
You've given so unselfishly
I couldn't ask for more.

You've given me such confidence
With all your wise advice;
The values you've instilled in me
Come from your sacrifice

Whenever things did not work out
And filled me with regret,
You challenged me to start again
And taught me not to fret.

You understood and gave me hope
As no one else could do;
In times of change, your love remains.
I owe my life to you !

The Empty Nest

Where have all the years gone?
How fast they passed me by.
I thought my life would never end,
And now I think and sigh.

I changed my children's diapers,
And kissed away their tears.
I told them bedtime stories--
What happened to those years?

There's nothing quite so precious
Than little hands held tight,
Then waving at the school bus,
As those hands fade out of sight.

I miss the homemade airplanes
And the special Valentine
That said, "I love you, Mommy.
Please, will you be mine?"

I loved to take my children out
And watch them as they'd play,
It seems I've hardly turned around,
And now they're on their way.

My son has grown to be a man,
My daughter's now a wife.
It seems like only yesterday
I gave them both their life.

I cherish all my memories, -
With children, I've been blest,
And pray for every one of them
As I dust their empty nest.

I'm so proud to be their mom,
They've accomplished much, I know,
And I can see my life fulfilled,
As I see their families grow.

by Arthur M. Pattison

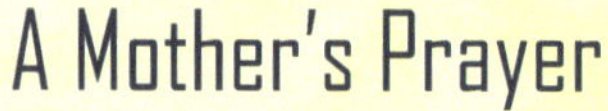

A Mother's Prayer

My hands were busy every day,
I didn't have much time to play
The little games you asked me to . . .
I didn't have much time for you.

I'd wash your clothes, I'd sew and cook,
But when you'd bring your picture book
To have me read and hold you near . . .
I'd say, "A little later, dear."

I'd tuck you in all safe at night
And hear your prayers, turn out the light,
Then tip-toe softly out the door . . .
I wish I'd stayed and played some more.

For life is short, the years rush past,
And little ones grow up so fast!
No longer are you at my side,
Your precious secrets to confide.

Now all your books are put away,
There are no children's games to play,
No good night kiss, no prayers to hear . . .
That all belongs to yesteryear.

My hands, once busy, now lie still,
The days are long and hard to fill;
I wish I might go back and do
The little things you asked me to.

I called you up the other day,
To see if you could come and stay.
"I'd be so glad if you could come . . .
"You said, "A little later, Mom."

"Dear Heavenly Father up above,
Assure me of your Heavenly Love.
Forgive me for my foolish ways,
And guide my children all their days."

Adapted by A. M. Pattison
from a poem by Alice Chase

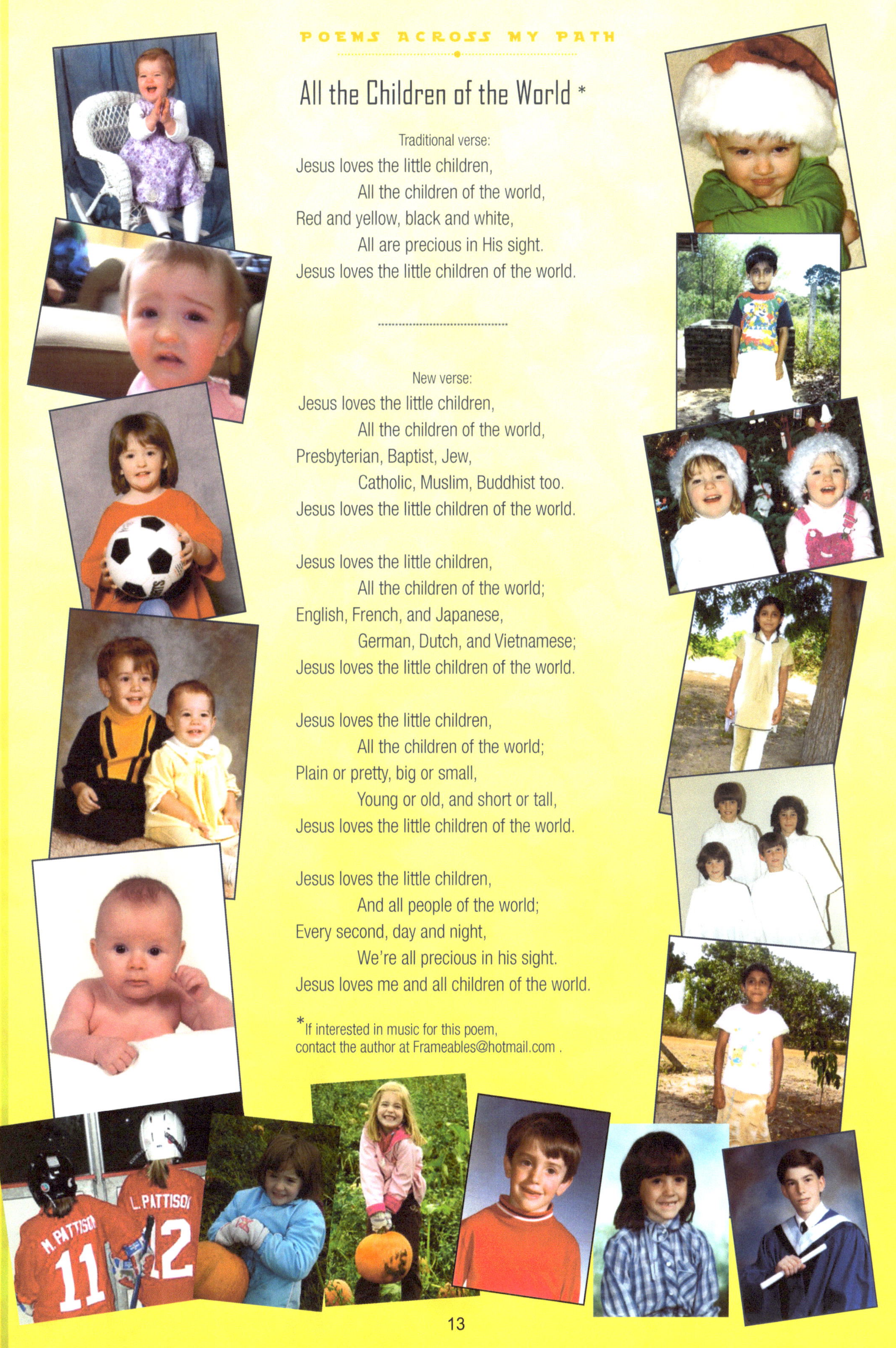

All the Children of the World *

Traditional verse:

Jesus loves the little children,
All the children of the world,
Red and yellow, black and white,
All are precious in His sight.
Jesus loves the little children of the world.

New verse:

Jesus loves the little children,
All the children of the world,
Presbyterian, Baptist, Jew,
Catholic, Muslim, Buddhist too.
Jesus loves the little children of the world.

Jesus loves the little children,
All the children of the world;
English, French, and Japanese,
German, Dutch, and Vietnamese;
Jesus loves the little children of the world.

Jesus loves the little children,
All the children of the world;
Plain or pretty, big or small,
Young or old, and short or tall,
Jesus loves the little children of the world.

Jesus loves the little children,
And all people of the world;
Every second, day and night,
We're all precious in his sight.
Jesus loves me and all children of the world.

* If interested in music for this poem,
contact the author at Frameables@hotmail.com .

Mama, Take My Hand

When I was just a little tot,
Trying hard to stand,
I looked around and had to say,
"Mama, take my hand."

So many times I tried to walk,
But on my seat would land,
But you were always there to say,
"Mama take your hand."

And when at last I started school,
As scared as scared could be;
You were there when I would cry
"Mama, stay with me."

Then when I started dating boys,
And wanted to be free,
I said so full of confidence,
"Mama! Let me be!"

But when the right man came along,
And with a wedding band,
I could hardly wait to say,
"Mom! He wants my hand!"

Then when I married and began
A family of my own.
You were there and said to me,
"Your Mama, you can phone."

So many times I called on you,
To solve a family fight,
And many times I realized that,
Mama's ways were right.

When tragedy came to our home,
I knew you'd understand,
That's why I asked you once again,
"Mama, hold my hand."

The busy years have come and gone,
My children are all grown;
And now I know why you have said,
"Your Mama's all alone."

Oh Mama come and live with me,
For you can barely stand,
And you can trust me when I say,
"Mama, take my hand."

by Arthur M. Pattison

My Grandpa

I like to walk with Grandpa,
His steps are short as mine.
He doesn't say, "Now hurry up!"
He always takes his time.
Most people have to hurry,
They don't seem to be free.
I'm glad that God made Grandpas,
Unrushed and fun, like me.

Adapted by A. M. Pattison

Hey, Grandma

Hey Grandma, can I visit you,
And bring with me Winnie the Pooh?
I like when you hold me,
And the stories you told me
That help me to know what to do.

Hey Grandma, please help me to grow,
And learn what direction to go,
So I can be strong,
When things seem all wrong,
From all of the things that you know.

Hey Grandma, I'd like your advice;
My girlfriend sure looks pretty nice.
I'd like you to meet her,
She'd like you to greet her,
And assure us true love will suffice.

Hey Grandma, now that I'm grown,
With children all of my own.
I help them be strong,
When things seem all wrong,
In just the same way I was shown.

Hey Grandma, come live with us too,
And bring back my Winnie the Pooh.
We all want to hold you,
We all want to love you
And help you to know what to do.

by Arthur M. Pattison

How Dare I Whine

I saw a girl upon a bus, who had such golden hair
I looked at her and sighed and wished, that I was just as fair.
But when she rose up from her seat, and hobbled down the aisle.
She had one leg and used a crutch, - and yet she had a smile !
Oh, God, forgive this heart of mine,
I have two legs, how dare I whine !

I stopped to buy some candy from, a man who had great charm
I wished I had his sweet rapport, as he offered me his arm;
And as I left, he said to me, " Thanks, you've been so kind;
It's nice to talk with folks like you, - most don't, because I'm blind !"
Oh God forgive this heart of mine,
I have two eyes, how dare I whine !

Then walking down the street I saw, a child with eyes so blue,
He stood and watched the others play, not knowing what to do.
I stopped a moment and then asked, "Why don't you join them, dear?"
And when he stared without a word, - I knew he could not hear !
Oh God, forgive this heart of mine,
I have two ears, how dare I whine !

With feet to take me where I'd go, and eyes to see the sunset's glow,
With ears to hear the trumpet blow, a mind to learn what I should know,
I lust for gifts and often fret, for things I think I need to get,
I am so rich, I oft' forget, - how much I'm always in Your debt !
Oh God, forgive this heart of mine,
I'm blessed indeed, how dare I whine !

Adapted by A. M. Pattison

Don't Quit

When things go wrong as they sometimes will,
And the road you're trudging seems all up hill,
When the funds are low and the debts are high,
And you want to smile but you have to sigh,
When care is pressing you down a bit . . .
Rest if must, - but don't dare quit.

Life is uncertain, with twists and turns,
As every one of us sometimes learns;
But don't fill your life with regrets about
What might have been had you stuck it out;
So never give up though the pace seems slow,
You could succeed with another blow.

Success is failure turned inside out,
The silver tint on the clouds of doubt;
It may be near when it seems so far,
You never can tell how close you are;
So stick to the fight when you're hardest hit,
When things seem worse you must not quit!

Great books have been written and fill many shelves
How the Lord helps those that help themselves,
Yet sometimes we need to be quiet and pray
For the wisdom and guidance to follow His way,
For then all the power and strength that we need
He'll give to inspire us and in His name succeed.

Adapted by A. M. Pattison

Success

If you think you're beaten, you're done,
If you think you dare not, you don't;
If you'd like to win,
But you're afraid to begin,
It's almost a cinch that you won't.

If you think you'll lose, you're behind,
For out in the world you'll find,
Success will begin
When you want to win;
It's all in your state of mind.

Life's battles aren't won with a plan,
Or a stronger or faster man;
They go to the one
Who once he's begun,
Keeps trying and thinking he can.

So never give up on your scheme,
Though hard the journey may seem;
When the road gets rough
The winners get tough
And focus again on their dream.

But never forget where to aim,
For success is not money or fame;
When the die is cast
The things that will last
Are the deeds that are done in God's name.

Adapted by A. M. Pattison

Serenity Prayer & Encores

GOD grant me . . .
The Serenity to accept
the things I cannot change,
The Courage to change
the things I can, and
The Wisdom to know the difference.

****

GOD grant me . . .
The Integrity to accept truth
from unfriendly critics,
The Insight to see talents
in unlikely people, and
The Grace to share with them.
GOD grant me . . .
The Security to listen to
those who disagree with me,
The Sensitivity to feel for
those who are hurting, and
The Humility to serve them.
GOD grant me . . .
The Power to accept
those who reject me,
The Patience to work with
those who use me, and
The Love to forgive them.

Adapted by A.M.Pattison

Bless This House

Bless this house, as we come and go;
Bless this house, as the children grow;
Bless our friends when they enter in;
Keep us safe and free from sin.
Amen

by A. M. Pattison

****

A Mealtime Prayer

Our Heavenly Father, we pause to pray
And thank you for our food today,
For sun and rain to make it grow,
And those who have prepared it so;
Help us to share with those in need,
And follow you in word and deed.
Amen

by A. M. Pattison

A Bedtime Prayer

Now I lay me down to sleep,
I pray the Lord my soul to keep;
Guard my family, night and day,
And lead me in your heavenly way.
Amen

by A. M. Pattison

Solomon asked for Wisdom

God also gave him riches and a long life;
I asked for Patience and God gave me problems;
I asked for Success, and God gave me perseverance;
I asked for Courage, and God gave me opportunities;
I asked for Strength, and God gave me a chance to grow;
I asked for Faith, and God gave me trials and temptations;
I asked for Love and God gave me troubled people to help:
I asked for Wealth, and God blessed me with children;
I asked for Peace, and God gave me his Holy Spirit;
I asked for Power, and God taught me to serve.

****

I received nothing I asked for . . .
Yet received everything I needed.

****

My God will supply all your needs
according to his glorious riches
in Christ Jesus. Phil. 4:19

Ten House Rules

Be constructive in your talk, with no gossiping.
Ephesians 4:29; James 1:26

Be co-operative, without complaining or grumbling.
1 Corinthians 10:10; Philippians 2:14

Be generous in looking after each other.
2 Corinthians 9:7,8; Timothy 6:17,18

Be truthful, and keep your promises to each other.
Proverbs 12: 22; Ephesians 4:15, 25

Be kind and forgiving to each other.
Ephesians 4:32; Colossians 3:13

Be helpful to one another, and bear each other's burdens.
Galatians 6:2; Ephesians 4:2

Be tolerant, especially of those whose faith is weak.
Romans 14:1; 15:1;2 1 Thessalonians 5:14

Be gentle, patient, and compassionate with each other.
Philippians 2:1,2; Colossians 3:12

Bon't let the sun go down upon your wrath.
Psalm 4: 4; Ephesians 4:26

Bove one another from the heart, for love fulfills the law.
Romans 13: 10; 1 Peter 1:22

Adapted by A. M. Pattison

A Teacher's Prayer

I want to teach my students more
Than lessons in a book,
I want to teach them deeper things
That people overlook;

The value of a rose in bloom,
Its use and beauty, too,
A sense of curiosity,
To find out what is true;

How to think and how to choose
The right above the wrong,
How to live and learn each day
And grow up to be strong;

To teach them always how to grow
In wisdom and in grace,
So they will someday make the world
A brighter, better place.

"Lord, let me be a friend and guide
To give these minds a start,
Upon their way down life's long road,
For then I've done my part."

Adapted by A. M. Pattison
from a poem by Jill Wolf

In twenty years will it really matter...

Who I outranked or outscored,
What kind of clothes or car I owned,
Where I lived or vacationed,
Why I worked so much overtime,
When I was able to retire, or
How much money I had in the bank?

****

But what will really matter is
If the world might be less wild
Because I was important
In the life of just one child.

Adapted by A. M. Pattison

Hugs

There's something in a simple hug
That always warms the heart,
It makes us feel we're home again;
When we've been far apart.

A hug's a way to share the joy
And sad times we go through,
Or just a way for friends to say
They like you 'cause you're you.

Our hugs are meant for any one
For whom we really care,
For grandmas, friends, and neighbours,
Or a cuddly teddy bear.

A hug is an amazing thing,
It's just the perfect way
To show the love we're feeling
When words are hard to say.

It's funny how a little hug
Makes every one feel good;
In every land and language
It's always understood.

A hug won't need to be repaired
With a battery or new part;
By opening up our longing arms
We open up our heart.

Adapted by A. M. Pattison
from a poem by Jill Wolf

Educating Our Youth

I dreamt I stood in a studio
And watched two sculptors there;
The clay they used was a young child's mind
And they skilfully worked with care.

One was a teacher, - the tools she used
Were experience, text books, and art;
The other, a parent, with equal skill
Used character, patience, and heart.

Day after day the teacher worked
With grace and a velvet glove;
And night after night the parent showed
Support, acceptance, and love.
And when at last their work was done

They were proud of what they'd wrought;
For the things they'd moulded into their child
Could never be sold or bought.

The child had knowledge, and skills to find
Resources for all of his needs;
But also the will to work with his peers
To seek Truth wherever it leads.

Both teacher and parent could easily see
That each had not done it alone;
For with the parent there was the school
And with the school was the home.

Whenever the School and parent agree
On the Source of all Life and Truth,
God will honour and bless their work
In educating their youth.

Adapted by A. M. Pattison

His Way

(The High Way)

And now, the end is near,
And so I face the final curtain,
My friends, I'll say it clear,
I'll state the case, of which I'm certain.
My LORD has died for me,
I trust in Him along life's highway,
Because, He set me free,
I'll walk in His way.

Regrets, I've had a few,
But now in Christ, a new relation,
For He will see me through
All of life's trials and tribulation,
We walk in sweet accord
Each careful step, along the highway.
Because, He is the LORD,
I'll walk in His way.

Yes there are times, I'm sure you know,
When I don't know the way to go,
But through it all, when there is doubt,
I turn to Him, He works it out.
Because He hears me when I pray,
I'll walk in His way.

I've loved, I've laughed, and cried,
I've had my fill, my share of losing,
I now in faith abide,
And rest in His own choosing.
To think He loves me so,
And I will go to heaven some day,
That's why, I love him so,
And walk in His way.

For what is a man, what has he got?
If just himself, then he is nought!
But God redeems, restores, and heals
The stubborn pride of one who kneels;
The Bible shows, God blesses those,
Who walk in His way.

Adapted by A M Pattison and Wm Nesbitt from a poem by Gilles Thibault and sung by Paul Anka (a school-mate of Art's at Broadview Ave School)

When I Am Gone

When I am gone, please let me be,
You still have much, to do and see;
You must not think of me with tears,
Be thankful for our many years.

We never suffered loneliness
Our years were filled with happiness;
I thank you for the love you've shown,
But now you must go on alone.

You gave such love and strength to me,
T' would be a shame to not be free.
So grieve for me a while, - but then
Get up! Go out! and Live again!

Yet only for a while we'll part,
So keep our memories in your heart;
I won't be very far away,
For near you always, I will stay.

Adapted by Arthur M. Pattison

Don't Weep For Me

Do not stand at my grave and weep,
I am not there, I do not sleep;
I am a thousand winds that blow,
I am the diamond glints on snow,
I am sunlight on ripened grain,
I am the gentle autumn rain.

When you awake in morning's hush,
I am the swift uplifting rush
Of birds that fly in circled flight
And soar 'mid stars that shine at night;
With angel choirs around His throne,
I bring you hope, - you're not alone.

So do not stand at my grave and cry,
I am not there, I did not die,
For when my race on earth was run
And all my trials and tests were done,
The Lord Creator came for me,
I reign with Him and watch o'er thee.

Adapted by A. M. Pattison

A LOVE STORY

Born in Ottawa in 1940, I graduated from Nepean High School in 1959, and from Carleton University in 1965. I then began a teaching career at Rideau High School in Ottawa. In October 1966, I met Freda Estabrooks at a Presbyterian Youth Weekend in Newmarket, Ontario, where I had been asked to be a Resource Speaker. I was immediately attracted to her. As I drove Freda to her billet's home that night, I asked her three big questions which were important to me at that time.

"Do you go to dances?"- a no-no for many narrow Christians. Her answer was "Just to Formals". Wow! Secondly, I asked, "Do you go to movies ?" - another no-no for many Christians in those days. Her answer was, "Just to Musicals". Amazing ! Then I asked the most important question of all, "Are you Calvinistic in your theology?" (- something most Christians knew nothing of, or if they did, were against it.). Her answer was, "Yes, I believe in Calvinism and predestination". (- a theology I had unsuccessfully tried to argue against during my years at university). I immediately knew she was the girl for me! (Unknown to me, when she joined her girl friend at her billet's home that night, she told her that she had finally met the man of her dreams.) The rest is history!

At that time Freda was teaching at an Elementary School in Toronto so we didn't see each other very often. However she came to Ottawa the following New Year's to meet my parents (just before my approving mother died). Later that month, I met her parents in Peterborough. Having previously obtained her father's approval, that February on our third date, on snow- shoes and in knee-deep snow in the chapel at Camp IAWAH (near Westport, Ontario), I asked her to marry me. To my delight, she agreed !

We were married the following August 27th 1967 in Peterborough. After a week's honeymoon in the Laurentians, she began teaching at an Elementary School right next to the High School at which I was teaching in Ottawa. After two more years, we moved to Toronto where I enrolled at the University of Toronto's Knox College. Freda happily financed my three years of theological studies by teaching at a downtown school in Toronto. Upon graduating in 1971, we accepted a call for me to be the minister at Essa Road, Barrie and Stroud Presbyterian Churches, North of Toronto.

Three years later we returned to Ottawa where I became an Assistant minister at St Andrew's Presbyterian Church. After two years, with a degree of disillusionment with Church polity and theology, I returned to teaching Math and Science in various Ottawa High Schools for the next 25 years, - still remaining active in church work, doing pulpit supply, with occasional marriages and funerals.

Over the last 45 years that we have been married, we have been blest with four wonderful children (an Executive in a well known drug company, an Aerospace Engineer, a Teacher and mother, and a co-owner of a small computer company designing web-sites). After the youngest was well along in elementary school, Freda was able to obtain an occasional and then a permanent teaching position with the school our children attended, the Ottawa Roman Catholic Separate School Board. She taught there for 15 years before retiring in 2003.

Since then, Freda has been diagnosed with Alzheimer's Disease. We have been lucky enough to have gone on several cruises, as well as tours of Israel, Turkey, Greece and Crete. We continue to enjoy our golden years, but struggle together with Freda's growing short-term memory problems. However, this terrible disease has not affected her wonderful, gracious, warm and bubbly personality. Freda continues to complete my life as a wonderful source of love, affection, and inspiration.

www.ingramcontent.com/pod-product-compliance
Ingram Content Group UK Ltd.
Pitfield, Milton Keynes, MK11 3LW, UK
UKHW060122300726
14090UKWH00002B/323

* 9 7 8 1 4 5 3 5 1 2 0 2 9 *